LET'S TALK BUSINESS CREDIT

CREDIT GUIDE

ATNECIV RODRIGUEZ, MBA

LETS TALK BUSINESS CREDIT

Secured lines of credit to unsecured, and go from 30-day capped terms to multiple, limitless sources of CREDIT.

Copyright © 2021 Atneciv Rodriguez

Intended for educational purposes only. All rights reserved. No part of this book may be reproduced without prior permission of the copyright owner, except for the use of quotes in a book review.

First edition 2021
ISBN: 9798334506947
Independently Published

BEFORE YOU CAN ESTABLISH BUSINESS CREDIT, YOU NEED:

A registered business entity (an LLC or DBA). Keep in mind if you intend to Make your Sole Proprietorship/Partnership an LLC, you should wait to start building business credit until the business is an LLC. This is because the EIN is tied to a specific business structure and if you build business credit as a Sole Proprietorship/Partnership with a DBA, you'll have to change the business structure on everything (including the EIN) & which is a very tedious process.

Your Employer ID Number (EIN). You need this for tax purposes, and you also need it to open business bank accounts and obtain business funding. You can apply at this link anytime between 7 am to 10 pm EST on weekdays:

https://sa.www4.irs.gov/modiein/individual/index.jsp

Your Data Universal Numbering System (DUNS) number. This number identifies you with the Dun & Bradstreet credit bureau. You would want to obtain this number and use this number whenever you apply for business credit so you can start to build your business' business credit. To create your profile with Dun & Bradstreet and obtain your FREE DUNS number, go to

https://www.dnb.com/duns-number.html

Your Business Bank Account. It's crucial to open a dedicated Business Bank Account to not only keep business income & expenses separate but to keep a record of business finances. You'll need these financial statements when you apply for funding.

WHAT MAKES HAVING BUSINESS CREDIT IMPORTANT?

Credit can be a powerful asset for a business. While personal credit is frequently emphasized for its role in financial health, building business credit is significant for many reasons.

In certain cases, having a well-established business credit history may be crucial for overcoming various challenges. Even successful businesses often seek financial resources to support growth, expansion, or new ventures.

For entrepreneurs and business owners looking to establish or expand their companies, building credit is essential. Access to sufficient capital can enable businesses to invest in growth opportunities, hire staff, purchase equipment, and more.
In this article, we'll explore some reasons why building business credit is important.

Easier Access to Business Financing
One of the key benefits of establishing business credit is gaining easier access to financing and capital. By building a solid credit history, entrepreneurs may qualify for business credit cards, loans, lines of credit, and other financial products.

While the approval criteria for business credit cards can vary, a good credit standing generally improves your chances of approval. Lenders and financial institutions evaluate creditworthiness to assess the risk involved in lending to a business.

The range of credit options available to a business can be broad. However, a strong and positive business credit profile can increase the likelihood of securing funding with competitive interest rates and favorable terms.

Protection of Personal Credit Score
Separating business credit from personal credit can help safeguard your personal credit score. Business credit bureaus maintain separate credit reports specifically for businesses.

Establishing a robust business credit profile involves acquiring credit in your business's name and responsibly managing business debts.

Separation of Personal and Business Finances
Using business credit cards can help keep business and personal finances distinct. This separation can broaden the range of borrowing options for business owners, including business-specific loans and lines of credit. These options may offer more favorable terms and lower interest rates compared to personal loans or credit cards.

GROW YOUR BUSINESS WITH CREDIT

Business Growth and Expansion

Building business credit is essential for growth and expansion. As a company develops a positive credit history, it can more easily secure financing for various growth initiatives. Whether expanding into new markets, opening additional locations, or investing in new technologies, access to capital can be crucial.

Credit can act as a catalyst for growth by enabling businesses to seize opportunities that might otherwise be out of reach. With sufficient funding, companies can invest in research and development, marketing campaigns, infrastructure, and other activities related to expansion.

Investing in Staff

A business credit card or line of credit can provide the necessary funds to invest strategically in staff. This investment helps build a team that supports the business's growth and success. However, it's essential to manage credit responsibly and ensure that investments in staff align with your overall business objectives and financial capabilities.

Specifically, a business credit card or line of credit offers financial flexibility for:
- Hiring New Employees: As your business grows, you may need to bring on additional staff to handle increased demand. Credit can help cover the costs of recruiting, training, and onboarding new employees.
- Training and Development: Investing in staff training can enhance skills, productivity, and overall business performance.

- Business credit can finance training programs, workshops, seminars, or certifications that help employees gain new knowledge and skills, contributing to the business's growth and competitiveness.
- Recruitment and Retention Incentives: Credit can cover recruitment costs, such as job advertisements, headhunting fees, or background checks. It can also fund retention incentives, like performance bonuses or benefits packages, to attract and retain top talent.
- Expansion and Scaling: If you're planning to expand or open new locations, credit can support the hiring process for new ventures, cover initial salaries, and facilitate smooth scaling.

Marketing

Strategic spending on marketing can maximize impact, strengthen a brand, and drive revenue. A business line of credit or credit card can finance various marketing initiatives, such as:
- Advertising
- Promotions
- Trade shows, conferences, or events
- Market research
- Website development and optimization

New Equipment or Inventory

Upgrading tools, equipment, or technology can boost productivity and efficiency. A business credit card or line of credit can help invest in new software, machinery, or other resources that enable employees to perform tasks more effectively. These credit options can also be used for equipment or inventory purchases as part of an expansion plan or upgrade initiative. Additionally, business credit can be useful for replacing broken or outdated equipment and inventory.

THE DIY APPROACH

This tool book is designed to help you establish and build business credit on your own. If you decide to take this approach, besides the LLC, EIN & DUNS numbers, and your Business Bank Account, you will need the following items to make your business credible and raise your approval odds:

- Business Phone Number
- Business Email
- Professional Mailing Address (Virtual Address is fine; No home addresses or P.O. Box)
- A website with a Professional Domain name

Once you have these items, your business will be credible and easier to fund. If you lack the time and energy to DIY, You can enroll in a business credit and finance partner that can help you build business credit (Tiers 1-3) & and guarantee business funding.

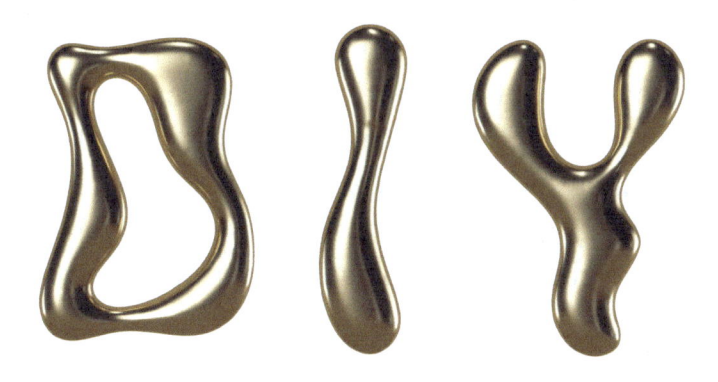

HOW TO BUILD A BUSINESS CREDIT PROFILE

Your business's ability to borrow depends on its credit profile and its <u>credit score</u>. Here is how to improve both:

1. Apply for an <u>Employer Identification Number</u> (EIN) through the IRS to help <u>separate your business and personal finances</u>.
2. Consider <u>forming an entity</u> such as an <u>LLC</u> or corporation, another step toward creating a separate identity for your business.
3. <u>Open a business bank account</u>.
4. Ask vendors such as big box home improvement and office supply stores to report your positive payment history to credit bureaus. Once you've built a history of paying these vendors on time, negotiate credit, such as the ability to pay them in 30 days.
5. <u>Apply for a business credit card</u> and make on-time — or early — payments.
6. Keep the percentage of the available credit you use to 30% or less. High credit utilization lowers your credit score.
7. Apply for a D-U-N-S (Data Universal Numbering System) number with Dun & Bradstreet. This unique nine-digit number lets the agency track your business's credit score. You usually don't need to apply to the other major bureaus in order for them to track your business's credit profile.
8. <u>Monitor your credit scores</u> and reports with credit bureaus to be sure their information is accurate, and to correct any errors. A high credit score can improve your chances of getting approved for credit and may lead to a better interest rate and repayment terms.

PAYDEX SCORING

Paydex Score	Explanation
100	Payment comes 30 days sooner than terms
90	Payment comes 20 days sooner than terms
80	Payment comes on terms
70	Payment comes 15 days beyond terms
60	Payment comes 22 days beyond terms
50	Payment comes 30 days beyond terms
40	Payment comes 60 days beyond terms
30	Payment comes 90 days beyond terms
20	Payment comes 120 days beyond terms
1-19	Payment comes over 120 days beyond terms

Your Paydex Score is a score (similar to a personal credit FICO score) that defines your business's creditworthiness. When building business credit, you need to be aware of both your personal FICO score, as well as your business' Paydex score.

Dun & Bradstreet says they require you to have at least 2 tradelines with 3 payment experiences each to generate a score, but according to NAV reports that you need at least three trade lines to get in the game. Make sure you always pay on terms or ahead of terms. You want a Paydex score above 80 and a FICO score above 690.

To keep track of your business credit score, you can open an account with NAV. They offer four accounts including a free account, but their $39.99 package will actually report your monthly payments as a tradeline to give you your first business tradeline.

To add this tradeline to your business credit, use this link:

https://www.nav.com/pricing-2/

SEVEN STEPS TO BUILD BUSINESS CREDIT

01 Formally Establish Your Business

02 Open Business Bank Account

03 Get a DUNS Number

04 Get a Business Credit Card

05 Establish a Line of Credit with Vendors and Lenders

06 Pay Bills on Time

07 Monitor Your Credit Reports

Fit Small Business

LINES OF CREDIT

A line of credit (LOC) is a loan arrangement that enables you to borrow funds up to a specified limit from a financial institution, such as a bank or credit union. You can access the funds as needed and only incur interest charges on the amount borrowed. Repayment can be made either in full immediately or through regular minimum payments over time. Since LOCs are considered open-ended debt, they do not have a fixed payoff date.

BUSINESS LOANS

Business loans provide an effective way to expand your business, make capital improvements and even consolidate or refinance debt using your collateral.

INTERNATIONAL TRADE LETTERS OF CREDIT

International trade letters of credit (LCs) are contractual agreements between banks that provide protection for both exporters and importers. An LC ensures that a seller will receive payment from the buyer's bank in a foreign country if specific conditions are fulfilled. To receive payment, the exporter must ship the goods and present the necessary documentation to their bank as proof.

Apply for a letter at Trade.Gov

HOW LENDERS MAKE DECISIONS

CHARACTER

CAPACITY

CAPITAL

COLLATERAL

CONDITIONS &

CREDIT SCORE

Character
- A subjective assessment of the business owner's personal history, including their credit history, legal judgments, and liens. This can also include their experience running a business, their willingness to learn, and their ability to pay their bills on time.

Capacity
- An indicator of the business's ability to repay the loan, including its financial capacity to cover operating expenses.

Capital
- Whether the business owner has invested their own money in the company, as well as any capital assets like cash or equipment that could be used as collateral.

Collateral
- Assets that the lender can use to secure the loan if the business can't repay it on time, such as inventory, accounts receivable, equipment, cash, or commercial real estate.

Conditions
- An assessment of the current economic climate and the purpose of the loan. This can include factors like industry trends, regulations, and competition. Lenders may also consider the borrower's plans for using the money, such as whether it's for expansion or to keep the business afloat.

Credit score
- Lenders typically consider both the business's and the owner's personal credit scores when making a decision. Higher credit scores generally indicate lower risk to the lender.

WHAT IS A GOOD BUSINESS CREDIT SCORE?

Perhaps the most common business credit score is the Paydex score, which ranges from 1 to 100. A higher score is better — which is true for most business credit scores but there are some variations among credit bureaus. Here's a breakdown of each:

Dun & Bradstreet issues several scores to evaluate elements of a business. The primary scores used are the Paydex score, failure score and delinquency score.

- Paydex score (1 to 100): Scores of 80 or higher are considered low risk, scores of 50 to 79 indicate moderate risk, and lower scores equal high risk of late payment.
- Failure score (1,001 to 1,875): A lower score translates to a higher risk for bankruptcy or business closure within 12 months.
- Delinquency score (1 to 5): A lower score is better because it equals lower risk for seriously late payment (91-plus days) or bankruptcy.

Equifax business credit scores
An [Equifax business credit report](#) offers three assessments for businesses: the payment index, the credit risk score and the business failure score.

- Payment index (0 to 100): Reflects past payment history. A higher score is better, with 90 or higher indicating bills paid on time.
- Credit risk score (101 to 992): Assesses the likelihood of your business becoming severely delinquent on payments. A higher score translates to a lower risk.
- Business failure score (1,000 to 1,880): Measures the likelihood of your business closing within a 12-month period. A lower score equals a higher probability of business failure.

Experian business credit scores

Experian's Credit Score report includes a business credit score and financial stability risk rating along with information like payment trends, account histories and public records.

- Business credit score (1 to 100): The higher the score, the lower the risk of serious payment delinquencies.
- Financial stability risk rating (1 to 5): A lower score is better because it represents a lower risk for default or bankruptcy in the next 12 months.

FICO business credit scores

FICO has just the one score, but it's important if you want an SBA 7(a) small loan (one that's less than $500,000). The SBA sets the minimum credit score for these business loans at 155, though preferred lending partners can approve applications below that threshold.

- FICO SBSS score (0 to 300): The higher the score, the less risk your business presents.

While the FICO SBSS has a set range, your business won't have a finite score. That's because creditors can adjust FICO's model to fit their institution's individual needs and risk tolerance. The FICO SBSS score includes information about both the business and the business owner.

SCORING MODEL

Scoring model	Score range
Dun & Bradstreet (PAYDEX score)	0-49: High risk 50-79: Moderate risk 80-100: Low risk
Equifax (Payment Index score)	1-19: Payments 120+ days overdue 20-39: Payments 91-120 days overdue 40-59: Payments 61-90 days overdue 60-79: Payments 31-60 days overdue 80-89: Payments 1-30 days overdue 90-100: Payments are on time
Experian (Intelliscore)	1-10: High risk 11-25: Medium-to-high risk 25-50: Medium risk 51-75: Low-to-medium risk 76-100: Low risk

One of the keys to a successful business today is utilizing and understanding

Business Credit

Your Business

Tier 1	Tier 2	Tier 3	Tier 4
Initial Business Credit	Advanced Business Credit	Bank Lending, Alternative Financing	VC, Bank, Investors

Foundation & Fundamentals

How Can **Tradelines** Help Your Business?

01 Credit Approval

02 Lower Interest Rates

03 Business Insurance Discounts

04 More Business with Good Payment History

TIER 1 TRADELINES

Once you have established your business entity and your business credit profile, and once you have opened your business bank account, you can start to build business credit through vendor tradelines. You want to attain 3-5 vendor tradelines and build for about 2-3 months. The tradelines listed in my 75 Business Tradelines & Funding Sources offer products or services that you may need in your business. You would purchase these items from these vendors on "Net 30 terms" which means you'll have 30 days to pay off the purchase(s). Don't just pay on time - pay early. Don't pay immediately but pay after 15 or 25 days so that your Paydex score would be established and maintained at 80+.

Secured Loans, (also part of Tier 1 Credit - build this for 2-3 months) from banks and fintech companies are a great way of building your business credit QUICKLY! You can use money, real estate, & more to secure your business loan. You invest with your own collateral so that the lender knows there's very little risk of default. These loans typically have lower interest rates, higher funding limits, and longer repayment terms (although it can take a longer amount of time to receive secured loan approvals.)

Secured funding is available via a Line of Credit or a Loan. Lines of Credit are revolving lines of funding while loans are not revolving (can only use up to the loan approval amount once). Most lending accounts have origination fees - a percentage associated with establishing a new account and processing a loan
application. This fee will typically come out of the loan itself.

LINES OF CREDIT

Name	Offers/Services	Annual Fee	PG	Credit Check	Reports to	Notes
Creative Analytics	Digital services- website development, socialmedia marketing, management, graphic designs, logos, etc	$79.00	No	No	Equifax and Account	Up to $10,000 Net 30 approvals. Must not have any derogatory business reporting (delinquencies). Must have EIN & DUNS. Apply: https://creativeanalyticsdc.com/net30/
Nav Business Boost	Full business and personal credit reports	$39.99/mo	No	No	D&B, Experian, business credit bureaus. and Equifax	Monthly subscription fee is reported to the business credit bureaus. Automatic approval as long as you have a registered business & EIN. Apply: https://www.nav.com/pricing-2/
The CEO Creative	Digital services (website development, graphic designs, etc.), printing services, office and cleaning supplies, & electronics.	$129.00	No	No	D&B, Equifax, and Credit Safe	Select Business Boost Package Up to $6,500 Net 30 Account approvals. Starter accounts typically receive $1,100 on approval, and after 90 days and 2 placed orders, you can request a limit increase and receive up to $6,500 in available credit. Apply: https://theceocreative.com/business-net-30-account/
Wise Business Plans	Build business plans for small businesses, non-profits, franchises, etc. They also create pitch decks, presentations, and more.	$99.00	No	No	D&B, Experian, and Equifax	Limits vary but initial applicants can receive between $1,850 to $5,000. Business must be atleast 30 days old with no derogatory business reporting (delinquencies). Wise Business Plan purchases are on Net 30 terms but are paid for with 50% due up front and 50% due before releasing the draft. Apply: https://wisebusinessplans.com/wise-net-30-account/

Vendor	Products	Cost	?	?	Reports to	Notes
Uline	Business operating supplies such as office supplies and furniture, shipping boxes, and food service supplies.	$ -	No	No	D&B and Experian	Limits vary. There are a couple of ways to get approved for Net-30 terms. Uline typically sends out a catalog and if you receive one of their large "brochures," you can use your customer number from the back of your catalog when prompted at checkout. Select the Net 30 billing option during the process and if the payment goes through, then you have been approved. Alternatively, you can use that customer number to apply using this form https://www.uline.com/CustomerService/ULINE_FAQ_Ans?FAQ_ID=104 (Call 877-513-3205 for questions about filling out the form). You can also call 1-800-295-5510 to set up an account and request terms, and upon approval they can provide a limit.
Quill	Office supplies, cleaning, paper ink and toner products.				Dun & Bradstreet	Up to $500- $1,000 Net 30 account approval. If you already have some business credit, you may be approved for more. Apply: https://www.quill.com/ At checkout select the 'Invoice My Account' option. They require an initial purchase and once you have an account they report QUARTERLY (not monthly) to Dun & Bradstreet. No annual fee but they recommend you to purchase a minimum of two or more orders in your first month (over $45). Then during the second month, they recommend you place larger orders of at least a $100 order, per week. Place even larger orders during month three.

Vendor	Description	Price			Details
Grainger	Tools, office supplies, industrial supplies, and much more to meet your business needs.	$ -	No	No	Dun & Bradstreet -Up to $500- $1,000 Net 30 account approval. You can go to https://grainger.com/ to create your online account to store shipping and invoicing details, but you'll need to call 800-GRAINGER (472-4643) to set up your line of credit.
Shirtsy	Offers direct-to-garment on demand printing that allows you to customize, design and fulfill customer orders for T-shirts, business cards and other accessories.	$99	No	No	To get approved you'll need a business license (if your business requires one) as well as a bank reference. Experian, Businesses must be at least 90 days old. Must Equifax, not have any derogatory business reporting Credit (delinquencies). Apply: https://shirtsy.com/net-30-application/

Vendor	Description	Fee			Details
HD Supply	Offers appliances, fitness and exercise equipment, healthcare supplies, janitorial, linens, paint and supplies, office supplies, food service equipment, HVAC, and more.	$ -	No	No	Credit limit varies and you can request the limit Dun &you are looking for in the application. No annual Bradstreet fee. Apply: https://hdsupplysolutions.com/s/credit_application or call 1-800-431-3000 for customer service.
Crown Office Supply	Office supply vendor, from stationary to electronics. Stationery, writing utensils, filing cabinets, and other materials you might need to use in the workplace or in a classroom.	$99	No	No	Annual fee counts as a payment reported on your D&B, business credit. Has a referral program with Experian, you can earn $15 per referral. Apply: Equifax, https://crownofficesupplies.com/net30-application/

Vendor	Description	$			Details
Summa Office Supplies	Office supply vendor with the brands you know and trust - Bic, Scotch, Sharpie, and more.	$	No	No	Equifax or Up to $2,000 Net 30 account approval. No Dun & annual fee but $75 minimum purchase. Two Bradstreet tiers of accounts for you to apply for. Tier 1 accounts report to Experian and no personal guarantee is required. After some time with good payment history, you can graduate to
Strategic Network Solutions	Office supplies, computer - accessories and digital content including computer and information technology products	$	No	No	Tier 2, where payments are reported to Dun & Bradstreet and a personal guarantee IS Experian and required. Credit Safe Up to $2,000 Net 30 account approval. No annual fee; establish a business credit profile by making an initial $80 purchase, then selecting "Bill My Net 30" at checkout. Pay this off within 30 days (after they invoice you) and then you should be approved for $2,000. Register and Experian & apply: https://stntsol.com/register

Office Depot	Office Large chain office supply company Max offering everything from pens and paper to office furniture & electronics.	$ -	No	No	Your Credit limit varies. Net 20 account terms. Apply: can also https://business.officedepot.com Enter your request D&B information and a representative will reach out to reporting)you to further qualify and approve you. They prefer you to have some credit history or at least 3 years of business history to waive Personal Guarantee. The initial reporting to the credit bureaus can take up to 90 days, but after that, **it's every 30 days.**
Business T-Shirt Club	Offers wholesale on blank work apparel like t-shirts, sweatshirts, hats, sportswear, corporate apparel, outerwear, masks, and more. Printing services available as well.	$ 69.99	No	No	Credit limit varies but I've seen approvals of up to $5,000. Must become a Member of their website online, and on the members-only website you can shop premium brands. Apply: https://www.businesstshirtclub.com/page/join Become a member and then you can also become an affiliate (don't have to be a member), and make $20 per referral for every successful sign-up.

BEST TIER 1 BUSINESS CREDIT VENDORS TO BUILD BUSINESS CREDIT

1. WISE BUSINESS PLANS
2. QUILL
3. NAMYNOT
4. SUPPLYWORKS
5. RED SPECTRUM
6. HD SUPPLY
7. HOME DEPOT
8. BUSINESS T-SHIRT CLUB
9. STRATEGIC NETWORK SOLUTIONS
10. CREATIVE ANALYTICS
11. STAPLES
12. OHANA OFFICE PRODUCTS
13. JJ GOLD INTERNATIONAL
14. SUMMA OFFICE SUPPLIES
15. ULINE
16. CEO CREATIVE
17. CREDITSTRONG

BUSINESS LINE OF CREDIT

BUSINESS LOAN

- Variable Interest Rate
- Replenishes as you repay
- only pay for what you draw
- No prepayment penalties
- best for short term needs

- Requires monthly or weekly repayments
- comes with an approved limit
- can be secured or unsecured based on lender criteria
- can be used anytime

- Fixed interest rate
- Does not replenish
- Pay back entire lump sum
- Early repayments may be penalized
- Best for long term needs

COMPARISON

CRITERIA	LINE OF CREDIT	BUSINESS LOAN
Repayment Schedule	Flexible	Fixed and pre-planned
Interest Rate (Based on Creditworthiness)	Starts at 7% to 9%	Starts at 1% to 2%
Fees	Lower fees depending on lender	High fee amounts and closing costs
More lenient	More lenient	Strict
Business Cash Flow	$100,000+ annually	$100,000 annually
Time in Business	1+ years	6 months to 1 year
Uses	Any purpose	May have limitations
Maximum Loan Amount	Around $250,000	$5+ million

SECURED LOANS

Name	Possible Loan Limit	Interest (APR) Origination Fee	Reports to	Notes
Wells Fargo Secured Credit Card	$500 - $25,000	11.90% on purchases and 20.74% on cash advances.	D&B, Equifax, and Small Business Financial Exchange, which Experian reports to all three major business credit bureaus.	Secured line of credit based on the collateral you put up - as much as $25,000. Your spending is reported to the Small Business Financial Exchange, which Experian reports to all three major business credit bureaus. They will pull your personal credit but there is no minimum score required. A Wells Fargo business checking or savings account must be open prior to applying for the card. Earn 1.5% cash back on qualifying purchases, earn 1 point on every $1 spent, and receive 1,000 bonus points every billing cycle when you spend at least $1,000 on qualifying purchases. There is no annual fee or origination fee with this account. Your account will periodically be reviewed for an opportunity to upgrade to an unsecured business credit card, and it will be based on your business and personal credit as well as your Wells Fargo card spending habits. Apply for the line of credit here: https://www.wellsfargo.com/biz/business-credit/lines-of-credit/

Name	Possible Loan Limit	Interest (APR) Origination Fee	Reports to Notes
Credit Strong Secured Loan	$ 10,000	5.83% to 14.89%	Equifax and Credit Strong offer a personal credit-builder account, and now they have PayNetexpanded to help build business credit. Their business loan requires no credit check to apply. The way it works is that they report a $10,000 loan to the Business Credit Bureaus and you can select a 60-month or 120-month plan to pay off this "loan." Keep in mind, that you do not have access to these funds during the loan payment - this is purely for you to build business credit. The good news is that the payments you're making actually go into a locked savings account and after the 60 or 120-month period (sooner if you pay it off sooner), you will have access to the account, minus the interest they charge to keep the account running. So after 60 or 120 months, you will have built up 5-10 years of business credit history with a $10,000 tradeline reporting. There is no penalty if you pay early and unlock your account early. You can choose your plan and get started here: https://www.creditstrong.com/business/build-business-credit-pricing/

Name	Possible Loan Limit	Interest (APR)	Origination Fee	Reports to	Notes
OnDeck Small Business Loan	$5,000 - $250,000	9.99% to 99%	2.5% - 4%	Experian, Equifax, Paynet	OnDeck offers short-term business loans that are secured by a general lien, meaning all your business assets are collateral for the loan, although they do not base loan approval on the value of your business. To be approved, you must have been in business for at least one year, have a FICO credit score above 600, and have $100,000 in annual business revenue. OnDeck does ask for a Personal Guarantee. Complete the application at: https://www.ondeck.com/short-term-loans and you can receive funds within the same day. You'll have 24 months to repay the loan and you will pay back the loan either daily or weekly.

Name	Possible Loan Limit	Interest (APR)	Origination Fee	Reports to	Notes
OnDeck Small Business Line of Credit	$6,000 - $100,000	Start at 35.9%		Experian, Equifax	OnDeck offers revolving lines of credit that are secured by a general lien, meaning all your business assets are collateral for the line of credit, although they do not base approval on the value of your business. To be approved for an OnDeck business line of credit, you must have been in business for at least 1 year, have a FICO credit score above 600, and have $100,000 in annual business revenue. OnDeck does ask for a Personal Guarantee. Complete the application at: https://www.ondeck.com/business-line-of-credit and you can receive funds within the same day. Interest rates start at 35.9% but only on the amount of financing used. There is a $20 monthly maintenance fee that OnDeck may waive for six months if you withdraw $5,000 or more within the first week of opening your credit line.

Name	Possible Loan Limit	Interest (APR)	Origination Fee	Report to	Notes
SBA Loans by SmartBiz	$30,000 - $5,000,000	4.75% - 7.00%	$3,000	Dun and Bradstreet, Equifax, Experian	Low rates, low monthly payments, and long terms are key aspects of SBA loans. An SBA loan is a small business loan that is guaranteed in part by the U.S. Small Business Administration and typically funded to you through a bank. Smart biz is an online lender assisting small businesses to apply for these loans through its network of preferred SBA lending banks and helps increase approval rates by matching small businesses with the bank most likely to say "yes" to their loan. The full process is described here: https://www.smartbizloans.com/how-it-works

The specific type of SBA loans offered are the SBA 7(a) loans for working capital, debt consolidation, and equipment purchases as well as SBA 7(a) loans for commercial real estate purchases or refinance. To qualify, you need to show at least $100,000 in annual revenue and be cash-flow positive. Also, you must have 2 years of business history on the books and a minimum credit score of 640. They do a soft pull first and then a hard pull once you are pre-qualified. You do have to provide a Personal Guarantee & a lien will be placed on your business assets. For all details and eligibility, as well as the application, click here: https://www.smartbizloans.com/faq

All one-time application and guarantee fees, as well as closing costs, are deducted from your loan proceeds at the time of funding. You should confirm with your lender which the business credit bureau(s) they report to, but most report to Dun and Bradstreet, Equifax, and Experian.

Name	Possible Loan Limit	Interest (APR) Origination Fee	Report to	Notes
Fundbox	Up to $150,000	Varies- 79.8%		A line of credit is repaid in 12 or 24 equal weekly installments — depending on the frequency you choose — plus a weekly fee. The fee varies based on your credit and also based on the plan you choose (12 weeks or 24 weeks). You can see how much you may pay in fees here: https://fundbox.com/pricing/ Must have been in business for just 3 months with $100,000 annual revenue. Must have a 600 personal credit score. *Even though they check your credit, they do not currently report to any credit bureaus.* So this is one line of credit that does not help you build your business credit but is an easy approval if you just need funds as a new business. You will have to connect your business bank account and/or accounting software to Fundbox so they can assess how much to approve you for in your credit. You can start the application process here and get funds the next day: https://app.fundbox.com/signup
	10.10 - 79.8%			

Name	Possible Loan Limit	Interest (APR) Origination Fee	Report to	Notes
BlueVine	$5,000 - $250,000	4.8% - 51% 1.50%	D&B, Equifax, and Experian	BlueVine offers invoice factoring services to help you finance outstanding invoices. Invoice factoring allows you to get advances (about 85% - 90% of the invoice amount) on those unpaid invoices due in 30, 60, 90 days or more. This gives you access to funds you need to manage and grow your business - for example, if you need to pay contractors or run payroll but don't have funds because you invoices haven't been paid yet. Invoice factoring would be a good option in that case. To qualify for BlueVine's Invoice Factoring, your business must have been in business for at least 6 months, have a Business to Business (B2B) model, with $10K monthly revenue. Must have a credit score of at least 530 but they do not perform a hard pull on your credit report. PG required & lien on business. You'll have to provide a bank connection or 3 months most recent bank statements. For all qualifications and to apply, go to: https://www.bluevine.com/invoice-factoring/

Name	Possible Loan Limit	Interest (APR) Origination Fee	Report to	Notes
Kabbage	$2,000 - $250,000	*Monthly* fees range from 0.25–3.50% for 6-month loans, 0.25–2.75% for 12-month loans, 0.25%–2.50% for 18-month loans		Backed by American Express National Bank. To qualify, you must provide a personal guarantee and have revenues of $50,000 annually or $4,200 per month over the last three months. Select businesses must also have an American Express business card relationship with at least 2 months of history. Find all eligibility rules here: https://help.kabbage.com/s/article/Applying-for-Funding

Kabbage Funding loans incur a loan fee for each month you have an outstanding balance. Monthly fees range from 0.25–3.50% for 6-month loans, 0.25–2.75% for 12-month loans, 0.25%–2.50% for 18-month loans. Very high interest because it's calculated monthly (rather than the usual annual percentage rate). Kabbage does not report repayment behavior to business credit bureaus or personal credit bureaus so it does not help you build business credit. Apply by clicking "Get Started" here: https://www.kabbage.com/line-of-credit/ |

Name	Possible Loan Limit	Interest (APR) Origination Fee	Report to	Notes
Currency Finance Business Loans & Equipment Financing	$150,000 - $5,000,000	Starting at 6% 0%		Currency is a FinTech companies and one of it's products, Currency Finance, offers both short-term and long-term business loans. Short-term loans can be as large as $2,000,000, and long-term loans can be as large as $5,000,000. although Currency's larger loan amounts can be a draw, they excel at financing smaller loans, offering a simple and fast application process for loans under $150,000 and funding in as little as 24 hours. Currency does not need you to have a high personal credit score, only a 620, and they will check your business credit history through Equifax Business, Paynet, and LexisNexis, but they won't require a minimum business credit score. For equipment financing loans under $150,000, all you'll need is an equipment quote to finalize funding. For their other loans, you'll need to provide 2 years of business tax returns, 6 months of bank statements, and more financial information. They require that all owners with at least 10% ownership provide a personal guarantee. Contact Currency Finance and start the application here: https://www.gocurrency.com/finance/ No info on if they report to any business credit bureaus.

BUSINESS LOANS

LOAN USES

- Working Capital
- Equipment
- Real Estate
- Inventory
- Startup Costs

LOAN TYPES

- Term Loans
- Line of Credit
- Real Estate Loans
- SBA Loans

SECURED LOANS
Loans **With** Collateral

vs

UNSECURED LOANS
Loans **Without** Collateral

HOW MUCH CAN A BUSINESS BORROW?

LOAN AMOUNT CALCULATOR

How Loan Will Be Used **+** Collateral Value **−** Down Payment

DETERMINING FACTORS

- Collateral
- Cash Flow
- Guarantor Strength
- Credit Score

HOW DOES THE LOAN PROCESS WORK?

1. Meet with Lender
2. Provide Documentation
3. Submit Application
4. Underwriting
5. Approval & Closing

HOW LONG DOES IT TAKE?

BUSINESS LOAN TIMELINES

- **Working Capital, Equipment, or Inventory Loans** — 3-5 Business Days
- **Real Estate Loans** — 30-60 Days
- **SBA Loans** — 60-90 Days

DETERMINING FACTORS

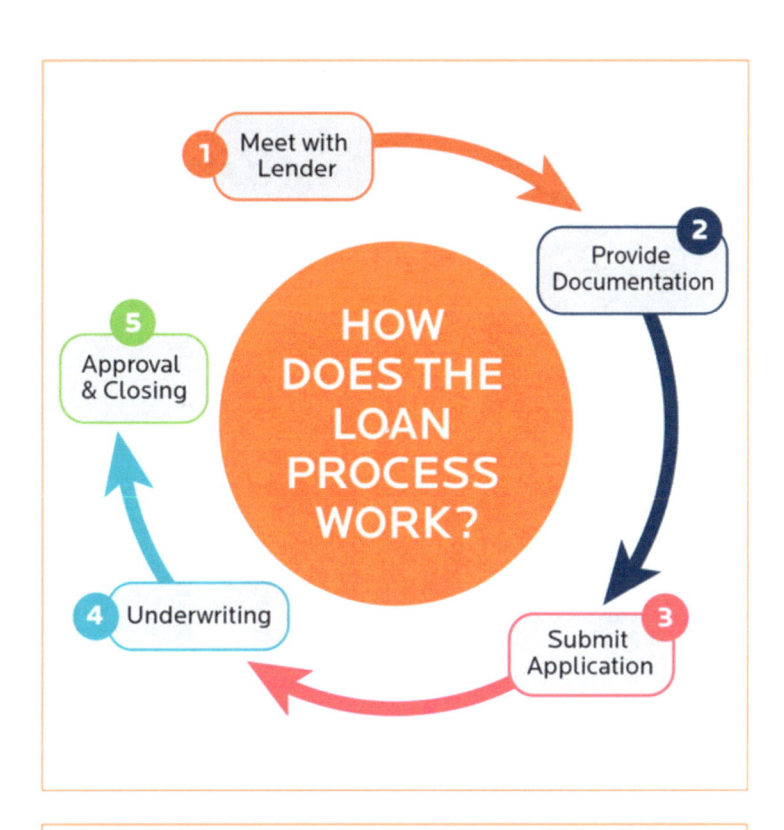

Documentation
Preparation and organization are key to a smoother and faster loan timeline.

Collateral
Loans secured with real estate generally take longer due to appraisals and title work.

Due Diligence
More complex loans require extra time during the underwriting process.

SECURED VS. UNSECURED LINES OF CREDIT: WHAT'S THE DIFFERENCE?

Secured

- Guaranteed by collateral, such as a home
- Guaranteed by collateral, such as a home
- Higher credit limit
- If borrower defaults, lender can seize collateral
- Example: Home mortgage or car loan

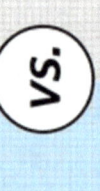

vs.

Unsecured

- Not guaranteed by any asset
- Higher interest rate
- Lower credit limit
- More difficult to get approved by lenders
- Example: Credit card

STREAMLINE YOUR SUCCESS: LOAN CHECKLIST

Basic Commercial Loan Checklist Template

Business Information:

Business Name: _____
Business Address: _____
Business Phone Number: _____
Type of Business: _____
Date Established: _____
Business Structure (e.g., LLC, Corporation, Sole Proprietorship): _____

Loan Purpose:

Purpose of the Loan: _____
Loan Amount Requested: _____

Financial Statements:

Last 3 Years of Business Tax Returns
Last 3 Years of Profit and Loss Statements
Last 3 Years of Balance Sheets
Cash Flow Statements for the Past Year

Business Plan:	Personal Financial Information (for each owner):
Executive Summary Business Description Market Analysis Organization and Management Sales Strategies Funding Request Financial Projections	Personal Tax Returns for the Last 3 Years Personal Financial Statements

Collateral:	Legal Documents:
Description of Collateral Value of Collateral Ownership Documents	Business Licenses and Permits Articles of Incorporation or Organization Partnership Agreements (if applicable) Any Existing Loan Agreements

Other Supporting Documents:

Business Credit Report
Personal Credit Reports for All Owners
Resumes of Key Management
Copy of Lease or Deed for Business Premises

TIER 2 TRADELINES

After you have generated a business credit score, you can start applying for Tier 2 vendors. Remember you need a score of 80+ to perpetually be qualified for these larger lines of funding. In Tier 2, you start with retail credit cards and then work up to cash credit cards. Build for another 2-3 months with the retail credit cards below. You want to have a total 8-10 reporting tradelines before you apply for cash credit cards. Retail credit cards consist of suppliers, retailers, fleet credit, etc.

The main difference between Tier 1 and 2 tradelines is that Tier 2 creditors will conduct a business credit check prior to extending credit to your business as well as a personal credit check. These credit grantors will issue higher credit limits and longer terms than Tier 1 Net-30 vendors.

Remember to use your credit lines regularly and pay your debts on or ahead of the due date so you can establish a strong business credit history and maintain that 80+ business credit score.

Once you've built your business' credit to at least 10 reporting tradelines and it's at a score of 80+ (usually takes about 6 months), you are ready to start applying for cash credit cards. You will build using these cards for another 1-2 months. With cash credit cards, both personal and business scores will be considered, so ensure your personal credit is at least 690 when you start to apply for cash credit cards. Most cash credit cards want you to have at least a "good" score which starts at 690. Keep in mind interest rates are higher if your credit score is low, as well as the credit limit for which you will be approved. The cards listed in my 75 Business Tradelines &
Funding Sources will typically not require a personal guarantee. They come with lots of rewards and interest will typically be lower. This is because the longer you're in business and the longer your business credit history is, the less likely you are to default on payments and therefore the less likely you are to be a risky decision for lenders.

TIER 2 TRADELINES

Name	Offers/Service	Interest Rate	Credit Score	Reports to	Notes
Home Depot Revolving Charge Card	Home Depot is a home improvement store with stores all over the country. They sell home decor, furniture, kitchenware, gardening tools, and more.	21.99%	670	D&B, Equifax, Experian	The Home Depot Revolving Charge Card is an in-store credit card that can be used nationwide at Home Depot stores. Citi is the managing bank of the The Home Depot Commercial Revolving Charge Card. There are some perks to having this card - for example you'll have one year to make returns (4x the length of Home Depot's usual return policy), and automatic enrollment to their Pro Xtra Paint Rewards program, which gets you discounts on paints, stains, and primers, plus additional paint-related perks like free job-site paint delivery. Additionally, Home Depot offers a Fuel Rewards program which saves you $0.10 in gas per gallon, at participating Shell and other select stations around the country. Apply here: https://www.homedepot.com/c/Credit_Center#RevolvingChargeCard

Name	Offers/Services	Interest Rate	Reports to	Notes
Apple Card	Apple is an electronics retailer. They sell phones, smart devices, computers, laptops, and more. You may have even heard of one of their most popular products... the iPod. :)	10.99% - 21.99% **Credit Score** 600	Bureaus	Make sure you select "Commercial Revolving Charge Card." Consumer The Apple Card is a MasterCard credit card which can be used at Apple Credit Retailers (online and in person) or at any location where MasterCard is accepted. While Apple Card does not have a business credit card option only(and therefore doesn't help you build business credit), solopreneurs and small business owners who use personal credit to fund business expenses can take advantage of the rewards and practicality the card offers. This card has NO FEES (e.g., no hidden fees, no annual fees, no late fees, no foreign transaction fees, no over-limit fees, no returned payment fees, no maintenance fees, etc.) and it breaks down your spending into color-coded expense categories. The credit card itself is literally a titanium card which is pretty secure because at a lot of places, you don't even have to take it out to pay. You can use Apple Pay! And when you do use your card, the card doesn't even have the card number there so there is less risk of fraud. To apply, visit:

Shell Small Business Card	Shell is a network of gas 700 stations and there are also participating Jiffy Lube's that offer vehicle maintenance services at which you can also use this credit card.	Experian	This Shell Small Business Card is accepted at over 14,000 Shell gas stations and participating Jiffy Lube locations nationwide. Multiple cards available for multiple employees. Earn rebates of up to 6 cents per gallon and obtain exclusive discounts at participating jiffy lube. To qualify, you should have a personal credit score of 700, but there have been reported approvals with scores as low as 620. To apply, go to: https://www.shell.us/business-customers/shell-fleet-solutions/shell-fleet-cards/shell-small-business-card.html
Costco Anywhere Visa Business Card from CitiBank	Costco is a membership club offers a variety of retail items in bulk: Anything from groceries to electronics to clothes to furniture. The benefit to this card is that it can in fact be used at any location Visa cards are accepted.	D&B, Equifax, Experian, Small Business Financial Exchange	You must be a Costco Member to qualify for the Costco Anywhere Visa Business Credit Card, so although there is no annual fee you must pay at least $55 to maintain membership with Costco. This card gives between 1% and 4% cash back on purchases (full details as well as application here: https://www.citi.com/credit-cards/citi-costco-anywhere-visa-business-credit-card). This card is eligible for use at Costco Wholesale Retailer or anywhere Visa is accepted.

| Lowe's Business Rewards from American Express | Lowe's is a retailer that 670 sells appliances, home goods, electronics, home improvement and construction tools, and more. This card can be used anywhere American Express is accepted. | 0% APR for the first six months and after that 15.74% – 24.74%. | Dun & Bradstreet | The Lowe's Business Rewards from AMEX Card can be used in US stores, on Lowes.com and LowesForPros.com, as well as at any store that accepts AMEX. With this card, you'll receive 5% off of all Lowe's purchases, 5x the points on purchases during the first 6 months, and a $100 credit to your statement upon approval. For all terms and to apply: https://www.lowes.com/l/Credit/business-credit-center Make sure you select the Business Rewards Card. |

| Amazon Business American Express Card | Amazon is an online retailer that sells just about anything you (or your customers!) might need. From books to bundles, Amazon has it all. | 14..24% - 22.24% | Dun & Bradstreet

Credit Score
700 | This credit card is available to any business owner with an Amazon account, even if it's not an Amazon Prime account. Great rewards being offered currently: $100 Amazon Gift Card upon approval, 1% - 3% cash back on purchases, and access to business-only pricing on Amazon products. Apply here: https://www.amazon.com/gp/help/customer/display.html?nodeId=GB8X9FFKT8FDF278 Make sure you select the Amazon Business AMEX Card (not the Prime Card; the Prime Card is for Amazon Prime members only) |

Dell Business Credit	Dell is an electronics retailer that sells computers, laptops, accessories, and everything your company may need! You can shop online at Dell.com and over the phone at 1-800-WWW-DELL.	Up to 29.49% D&B, Credit Score 640	Dell Business Credit is a revolving line of credit for your business' technology needs. Up to $50,000 in credit available. Account holders have access to exclusive offers which are all listed here: https://www.dell.com/en-us/work/lp/dell-business-credit#Promotions Minimum monthly payments are the greater of $15 or 3% of the new balance shown on the monthly billing statement. Apply for funding here: https://www.dell.com/en-us/work/lp/dell-business-credit
Race Trac Elite Card	RaceTrac has a network of gas stations (RaceTrac and RaceWay). Over 750 locations.	D&B	The RaceTrac Corporate Fleet Elite Card is a great way to manage your Experian commercial fuel expenses. You can obtain multiple cards for and Equifax employees, track those fuel expenses, and save up to 5¢/gal at RaceTrac and RaceWay. If your business is less than 3 years in business will need a PG. RaceTrac doesn't specify what minimum credit score is needed to qualify, however applicants should have a great credit record. Also no specified APR on purchases. Apply at: https://www.racetracfleetcard.com/fuel-card/racetrac-elite-fleet-card/

| Exxon Mobil Business Card | ExxonMobil company is a merger of gas station giants Exxon and Mobil. You can fill up or get select maintenance services at over 11,000 locations nationwide. | N/A | 24.00% variable | D&B | ExxonMobil Business Card is especially good for businesses on the East Coast as Equifax, there are more locations on East of the Mississippi. ExxonMobil's business card is Experian, through Citi Bank. While ExxonMobil does not advertise which business credit and SBFEbureaus they report to, Citi typically reports the positive payments on it's business accounts to D&B, Experian, Equifax, and the SBFE. They do not specify what personal credit score you need to qualify, however they do mention there is a credit check and a credit limit is based on your business and personal credit report. There are testimonials of entrepreneurs with a score as low as 625 getting approved, but line of credit at that score is around $300, so the higher the score the better. Interest goes up to as much as 29.99% if payment is late plus there is a late fee which is the greater of $29.00 or 2.50% of the account balance as of the payment due date. All Terms & Conditions are here: https://citiretailservices.citibankonline.com/CRS/acq/launch/index.action?app=UNSOL&siteId=PLOF_EXXONMOBIL&sc=20415#tnc Application and rewards are found here: https://citicards.citi.com/usc/crs/exxonmobil/business.htm?BTData=Mfx.B.B4f.J.BWT.KwB9.ZrZ.c9c.d7c.Bj.PP.uQ&ProspectID=B3964244206548EF9DEE59F525C13D04 |

Fuelman Deepsaver Fleet Card	Fuelman is a network of gas stations nationwide - there are 50,000 locations including name brands like Chevron, Sam's Club, Kwik Trip, and Wawa.	15% - 20%	D&B, Experian and Equifax	Fuelman offers a wide network of gas stations nationwide from trusted brands. They offer rewards such as saving 8¢ per gallon on diesel and 5¢ per gallon on unleaded at their almost 50,000 locations. Like the fleet cards mentioned before, this card also helps you track expenses, gives you alerts, and lets you add multiple employees. While there is no annual fee, there is a fee of up to $12 per card depending on the plan you book. There are three plans to this business credit card - Regular, Plus, and Premium. Compare all the plans and apply here: https://www.fuelman.com/card-details/deep-saver/ One thing I unfortunately have to note about this card is that they are notorious for hidden fees. Check your statements and try to pay attention to what additional fees may be there. Full terms & conditions.
			Credit Score 670	

Best Buy Business Advantage	Nationwide and online retailer Best Buy sells electronics, computer tech and more.	640	There are 900+ retail stores at which to shop, or you can shop over the phone with an Account Professional, or online at BestBuy.com. Competitive pricing on their products. All of your purchases through the Best Buy Business Advantage program will come with detailed net 30 invoices. For approval, Best Buy will look at your Experian Business Credit Profile and your personal credit. (No mention of what business credit bureaus Best Buy reports to) This is one of the few retail tradelines that prefers at least a year in business but if you have a substantial amount of tradelines already, definitely try to apply. Here is the link: https://www.bestbuy.com/site/bestbuy-business/best-buy- business-advantage/pcmcat1556029048796.c?id=pcmcat1556029048796 Tip: If you don't have at least 10 tradelines, don't request more than $5,000 in credit. Your credit limit will be based on your credit.

Name	Possible Credit Limit	Interest	Annual Fee	Min. Credit Score	Reports	notes
Capital One Spark 1% Classic for Business	$2,000.00	26.99% variable		580	D&B, SBFE	Easy approval business credit card that only requires a 580 Experian, score so it's very accessible to business owners who are still working on their personal credit scores. No annual fee, 1% cash back on every dollar spent. You can get approved for as much as $2,000. Reports to both business & personal credit bureaus. Lots of tools for business owners - an itemized list of expenses for tax preparation at the end of the year. See all of the card benefits here: https://www.capitalone.com/small-business/credit-cards/benefits/ and apply here: https://www.capitalone.com/small-business/credit-cards/spark-classic/

Name	Possible Credit Limit	Interest	Credit Score	Reports notes
American Express Blue Business Cash Card	$ 50,000.00	0% - 19.24%	690	American Express offers many credit card options and the Blue Business Cash Card is the best for building your credit. Credit Limits as high as $50,000. 0% intro APR onpurchases for 12 months from the date of account opening, and then 13.24% - 19.24% after that. You can earn a $250 statement credit when you spend $3,000 in purchases in your first 3 months. Note that if your account becomes delinquent that will be reported to the consumer credit bureaus as well. Full details and application here: https://www.americanexpress.com/en-us/business/credit- cards/blue-business-cash/

Card	Limit	APR	Fee	Score	Reports to	Notes
Chase Ink Business Cash Credit Card	$25,000.00	13.24% - 19.24%	$ -	690	D&B, Equifax, Experian, and SBFE	Chase offers three Ink Business Cards, and the one I'm specifically referring to here is the Ink Business *Cash* Card. You can obtain as much as $25,000 in credit from Chase through this card. The benefit of this card is that you can receive $750 cash back on this card, plus receive 1-5% cash back on purchases. There's also 0% intro APR on Purchases for 12 months and then variable interest fee of 13.24% - 19.24%. Pricing and Terms, including late fee details, here: https://applynow.chase.com/FlexAppWeb/pricing.do?card=GJ2N&page_type=appterms And you can apply here: https://creditcards.chase.com/a1/olainkcash/750
Kleer Card	$58,500.00	N/A	$ -	N/A	Dun & Bradstreet	Kleer (licensed through Sutton Bank) is a brand-new expense management platform that launched in January 2021. Besides expense tracking, Kleer also offers a business credit card "solution" for small businesses and non-profits. No PG, no credit check. Keep in mind, the card balance needs to be paid in full after 7 days or 14 days at most. Since they are relatively new, there is limited info on the amount of interest they charge, but there is certainly no annual fee. They do not specify how much their credit limit can be, however, I have seen approvals as high as $58,500. While there is no credit check, they do link your business bank account to their platform so they can authenticate it and use the deposits into the account as part of the decision process in deciding whether or not to offer credit, and if so, how much. When you apply online here: https://www.getkleercard.com you receive your credit limit and rewards info immediately.

Divvy Card	$ 50,000.00	N/A	$ -	550	SBFE	Divvy is another fintech company that offers cash credit on Net terms. You have to pay the full balance each month within 7, 14, or 30 days (no interest since you cannot carry a balance into another month). Get approved for as much as $50,000. Keep in mind if you get approved and you'd like a higher limit, you can actually counter-offer them for the amount you want and possibly even be approved for more. There is no hard pull, but you can opt into giving a Personal Guarantee (even though you do not have to). There is a soft pull from Experian Consumer Credit Bureau. If you do not want to personally guarantee the line of credit (and if you do not want a hard pull on your consumer credit report) then do NOT select "I want to PG (Personal Guarantee)." Here is the application: https://getdivvy.com/credit/ Pro-Tip: Fill out the application in incognito mode. Make sure you use the card within 90 days of opening, otherwise Divvy will close the account.

Brex Account & Credit Card	$ 100,000.00	N/A	$ -	N/A	D&B and Experian	Brex is a zero-fee banking alternative that offers instant approval for a business line of credit. Issued a virtual card immediately and then mailed a card as well. They give you a credit limit based on how much your business is making, rather than your personal credit - between $100 and $100,000. No minimum credit score or Personal Guarantee! Company equity is reviewed to prevent fraudulent activity. This is a charge card, not a credit card, meaning the balance is due in full each billing cycle, and you can't carry debt from one month to the next. That also means there is no interest on charges! When you sign up for the cash management feature, you can get your card limit raised. The account has no fees and allows you to send free wire transfers. Integrates with Quickbooks and other bookeeping softwares. Lots of rewards and up to 8x the rewards on certain purchases. All reward details as well as the application are found here: https://www.brex.com/product/credit-card/

BEST TIER 2 BUSINESS CREDIT VENDORS TO BUILD BUSINESS CREDIT

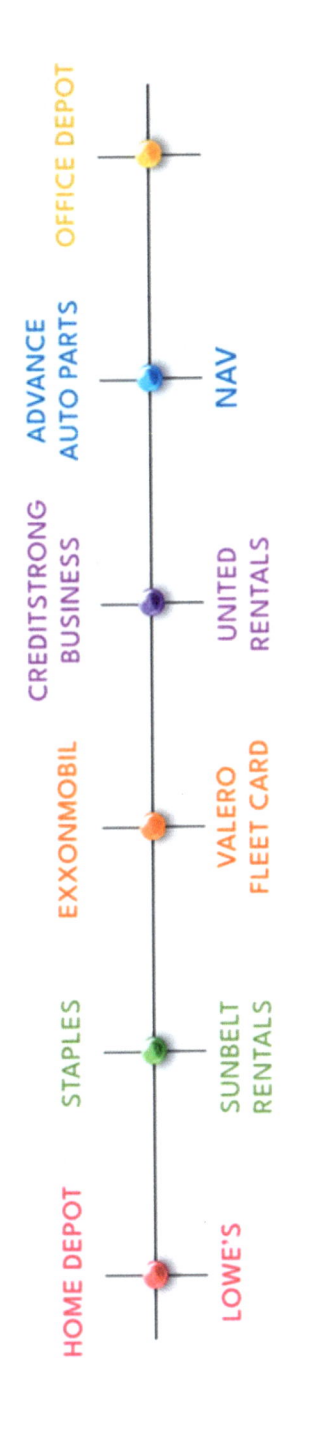

- HOME DEPOT
- STAPLES
- EXXONMOBIL
- CREDITSTRONG BUSINESS
- ADVANCE AUTO PARTS
- OFFICE DEPOT
- LOWE'S
- SUNBELT RENTALS
- VALERO FLEET CARD
- UNITED RENTALS
- NAV

TIER 3 UNSECURED TRADELINES

After at least 8-10 months of building business credit with vendor tradelines, secured loans, and lines of credit, you should be in good shape to start seeking a loan from a bank, fintech company, or online lender.

The Tier 3 list in my 75 Business Tradelines & Funding Sources specifically lists loans that are unsecured. They do not require any collateral or even a personal guarantee. These loans are either short-term, or long-term loans, larger lines of credit, equipment loans, vehicle loans, or commercial loans.

Loans can be used to expand your current business or start an entirely new one. For example, you can use a commercial real estate loan to open an Air B&B, or an auto loan to start a car lease business on Turo. Like any line of credit, remember to only borrow and use what you can pay back while still making a profit.

Name	Possible Loan Limit	Interest Score	Annual Fee	Min. Credit	Notes
PNC Small Business Line of Credit	$20,000 - $100,000	8.18% - 15.57%	$ 175.00	650	PNC Bank is a nationally chartered American bank based out of Pittsburgh, It has branches in 19 states and Washington, D.C. PNC offers secured and unsecured loans, but they also offer 3 kinds of revolving business lines of credit. Their Choice Line of Credit is unsecured, no collateral is required. Monthly payments are 1.5 percent of the balance (minimum of $100), plus an origination fee. There must be no bankruptcy claims on your business and no outstanding financial obligations. You must have been in business for at least 3 years and have at least 5 years of credit history. They are looking for a 650 minimum score and a 40% or less debt-to-income ratio. For a list of prohibited industries and to apply now, click here: https://www.pnc.com/en/apps/welcome-pages/business-lending-choice-credit-line-of-credit.html

Name	Possible Loan Limit	Interest Score	Annual Fee	Min. Credit	Notes
Chase Small Business Loan	$5,000 - $500,000	3-10% Varies		680	Morgan Chase Bank is a large bank with locations in over 39 states. Chase offers many loan options, with terms up to 7 years long. If you already have a business bank account, you can visit your local Chase bank to apply (an appointment may be required). Requirements may vary by branch. The annual fee varies from $150 - $250 depending on the loan amount, and there is a 1% to 5% origination fee. Get more info here: https://www.chase.com/business/loans/financing
Financing Solutions Now Line of Credit	Up to $100,000				The application process is super simple. You can get an offer letter immediately; processing time takes 48-72 hours. There are no origination fees and no fees at all until you use funds. A minimum credit score is not specified, as well as what exactly the fees are when you do use funds. To apply or receive a quote, call 862-207-4118 or visit www.financingsolutionsnow.com

Clearco (Formerly Clearbanc) Cash Advance	$10,000 - $10,000,000

Clearbanc advances come with a flat fee of 6% to 12.5% instead of interest. | | | | Clearco is an online lending platform that provides cash advances for your business, between $10,000 to $10,000,000. Decisions about whether or not you qualify for an advance are based on your business performance, so your credit score won't factor in. Your payments will also fluctuate based on how much revenue you're bringing in (based on a percentage of each transaction you make, between 1% to 20% of each sale), which can make it easier to keep up with paying back the money you owe during seasonal downturns. You must've been in business for at least 6 months, and be working in the eCommerce or Software industries. Your business must also have an average monthly revenue of at least $10,000. No annual fee is mentioned on their website. You can receive access to funds in 24 hours after you apply here: https://clear.co/landing/for-founders/?utm_campaign=2020_as_na_google_search_brand_mca_na_na&utm_content=2020_as_na_google_search_brand_mca_na_na_focused_bmm--clearco--516035157244&utm_source=adwords&utm_term=clearco&utm_medium=ppc&hsa_ad=516035157244&hsa_grp=121056557171&hsa_kw=clearco&hsa_ver=3&hsa_net=adwords&hsa_acc=3143805101&hsa_src=g&hsa_cam=1632587273&hsa_mt=p&hs a_tgt=kwd-298442824255&gclid=CjwKCAjwgviIBhBkEiwA10D2j5-Jk8YkkFui9Z0Mrl72NJYD3RlNKh_MvB4mJ0XlhjU_mm8vOq0ndBoCeKkQAvD_BwE |
| **Balboa Capital Loans & Equipment Financing** | Up to $250,000 | Varies | $ - | 560 | Balboa Capital is another online lender that offers loans, lines of credit, and equipment financing to small businesses. You can apply online and receive funding in days. For all lending offers, you need to have been in business for at least 1yr, with a minimum of $300,000 in annual revenue. For Equipment Financing specifically, you can have a minimum of $100,000 in annual revenue. Interest rates start around 9% to 10% and vary based on your qualifications. To apply, go to https://www.balboacapital.com/ and click on Funding Options to choose your offer. |

Lender	Amount	Rate	Fee	Credit	Description
Lending Club + Accion Opportunity Fund	$5,000 - $500,000	Varies	$ -	N/A	Lending Club is an online former lender who used to originate small business loans but stopped in 2019. Now, Lending Club matches those who apply through their website to the best loan offer through Accion Opportunity Fund, a non-profit lender that uses your fees to fund more businesses. To qualify for loans up to $500,000 (with up to 60 months payment terms), borrowers must have at least 12 months in business, $50,000 in annual revenue, and own 20% or more of the business. Also, you can't have any bankruptcies or tax liens. You can get a quote on monthly payments and interest fees here: https://www.lendingclub.com/business/ and you can also call your Opportunity Fund Client Advisor at (855) 846-0153, 7 days a week, 8 am –8 pm EST.
Capital One	10,000	5.9% to 18.65%	$ -	660	Capital One is the nation's 5th largest bank and offers many forms of financing for businesses. There are credit cards, such as the Spark 1% Cash card on my list of Tier 2 cash credit cards. There are loans for small businesses. To qualify for an equipment or vehicle loan from Capital One, you must have been in business for 2 years and have an open Capital One business checking account. The loan terms are also very flexible; this enables you to repay the loan easily for a maximum of 5 years without any hassle. The amount, interest rate, and term you get not only depends on your creditworthiness and ability to repay but the value and expected lifetime of the equipment you're purchasing. Connect to a Capital One banker and apply here: https://www.capitalone.com/small-business-bank/financing/equipment-vehicle-loans/

Loan	Amount	Rate	Fee	Credit	Description
Bank of America Commercial Real Estate Loan	Starting at $25,000	1.99%	0.75%	660	The Bank of America Corporation is an American multinational investment bank and financial services holding company. Bank of America has slowed down loan offers since the PPP loans rolled out in early 2021, but still allows you to apply for a commercial real estate loan with their institution to purchase land or real estate in your business name. On new credit applications submitted June 7, 2021 through September 30, 2021, there is a special 1.99% interest rate. There is also a 25% discount on loan origination fees with this promo, but both interest rates and origination fees vary on each loan. The upfront origination fee is 0.75% of the amount funded. You will have to call or go into a local branch to apply for a loan, but you can go ahead and book an appointment at your local branch here: https://www.bankofamerica.com/smallbusiness/business-financing/commercial-real-estate-loans/ Click "Get Started."
TD Bank Loans & Business Line of Credit	Limits between $100,000 - $1,000,000	Varies	N/A		TD Bank is a large bank with branches mainly on the east coast of the country. TD Bank offers a lot of lending products - from commercial loans to small business lines of credit. You can call 1-855-278-8988 to find out more about commercial real estate loans but most loans and lines of credit can be applied for online. If you apply for a line of credit under $100,000, you do not have to provide any tax or financial statements, and you can just apply online here: https://esecure.tdbank.com/net/sblending/ To qualify, you'll need some personal info about you, and then supporting documentation (LLC docs, Operating Agreement, and more). The process takes 3-6 months overall, so this isn't a good option for businesses that need access to capital quickly. They do not specify how much the origination fee is, or what the minimum credit score is, so feel free to call a customer service representative at 1-855-278-8988 before you apply. They are known for their excellent customer service.

CREDIT CARD REWARDS COMPARISON CHART

Cash Back	Points	Miles
Cards available with bonus cash back for specified category purchases	Cards available with bonus points for specified category purchases	Cards available with bonus miles for specified category purchases
Simplest to redeem	Can be co-branded or bank-specific	Can be co-branded or bank-specific
Rewards have set value	Value may vary with redemption option	Value may vary with redemption option
May be redeemed as a statement credit or deposit to an eligible bank account	Branded points are redeemable for specific merchandise or expenses	Branded miles are redeemable for airfare with specific airline
May be redeemed during checkout with some retailers	Generic points may be redeemed for cash back, merchandise, travel, events, & more	Generic miles may be redeemed for air travel, hotel stays, or other travel-related expenses
May be converted to points in some programs	May be transferable to an outside loyalty program	May be transferable to an outside loyalty program

TIER 4 INVESTORS

Tier 4 is a shift outside of institutional lending and commercial credit to the world of venture capitalists and private investors. Mature businesses are great candidates for private investors or Venture Capitalists.

Venture Capitalists are investors who are looking to invest in established businesses with a high return on their investment (ROI). They typically invest higher amounts than other investors, such as "angel investors."

An angel investor can help a startup company who needs financing at an early stage. Both types of investors will need a solid business plan with growth projections and ROI numbers. With multiple years of financials and a solid growth strategy, you can gain a funding source from a venture capitalist - as well as a great information resource as investors typically have experience - and with an outstanding business plan, you can gain funds from an angel investor before you try the venture capitalists.

Keep in mind that there are many stages of investment - from seed funding to Series C funding, but here we are focusing on investing on a general sense and diving more into detail on business credit and loans.

5 Things You Should Know About Business Tradelines

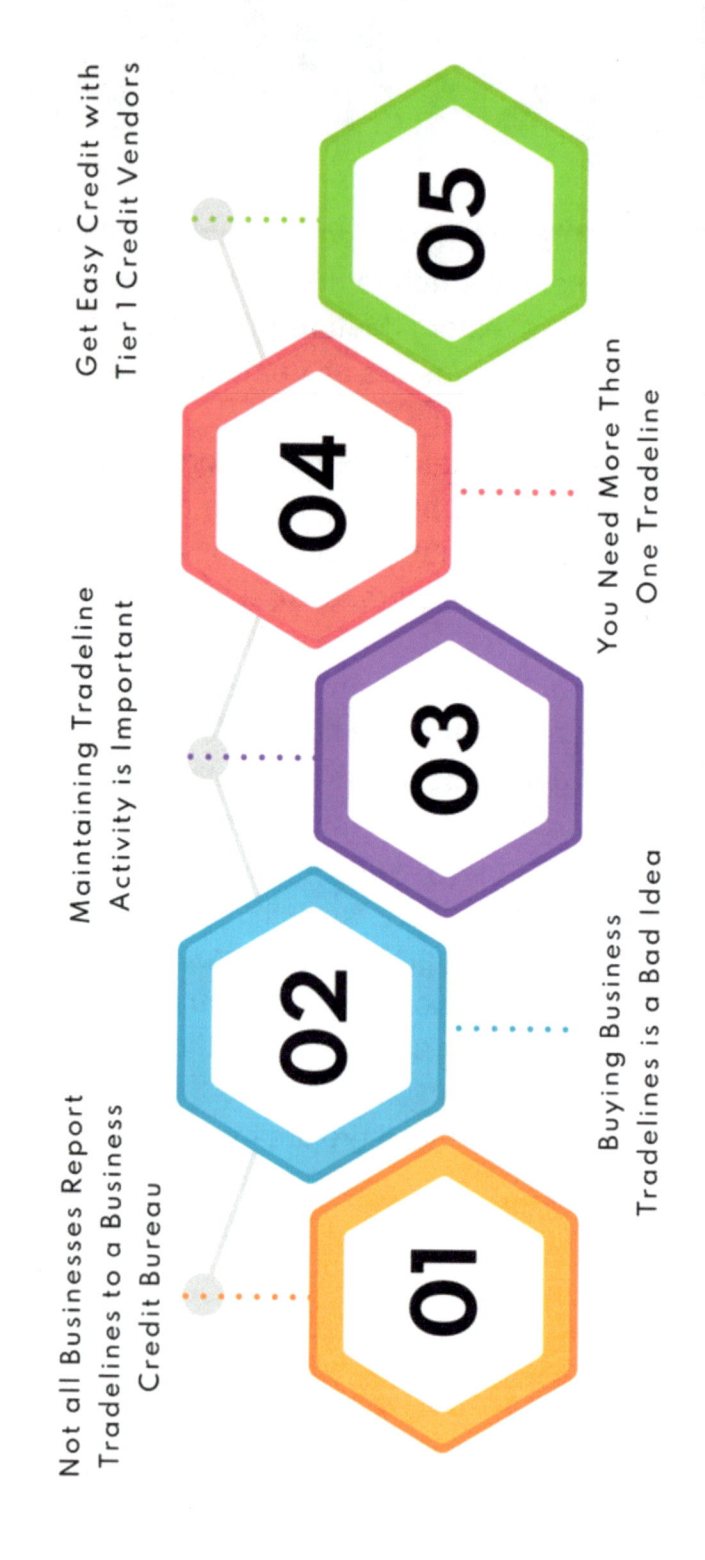

01 — Buying Business Tradelines is a Bad Idea

02 — Not all Businesses Report Tradelines to a Business Credit Bureau

03 — You Need More Than One Tradeline

04 — Maintaining Tradeline Activity is Important

05 — Get Easy Credit with Tier 1 Credit Vendors

Angel Investor Firms Website

Seed Invest https://www.seedinvest.com
Life Science Angels https://www.lifescienceangels.com/apply-for-funding
Tech Coast Angels https://www.techcoastangels.com/
Golden Seeds https://goldenseeds.com/
Hyde Park Angels https://hydeparkangels.com/
Angel Investment Network USA https://www.angelinvestmentnetwork.us/
First Round Capital https://firstround.com/
Techstars https://www.techstars.com/startups
Atlas Ventures https://atlasventure.com/
Republic https://republic.co/raise
Our Crowd https://www.ourcrowd.com/startup-application
Gust https://gust.com/

Venture Capital Firms Website

Crestmont Capital https://www.crestmontcapital.com/venture-capital
Advanced Technology Ventures https://www.atvcapital.com/
Uncork Capital https://uncorkcapital.com/
Cowboy Ventures https://www.cowboy.vc/
Initialized https://initialized.com/how/
Great Oaks Venture Capital http://www.greatoaksvc.com/
Index https://www.indexventures.com/
Bassemer Venture Partners https://www.bvp.com/

WHERE TO FIND GRANTS

Grants are funds awarded by corporations, governments, or non-profit organizations that you can use to fund your business without having to pay back the funds.

The federal or state government will typically disburse funds through those non-profit organizations (foundations) or through local agencies such as an Economic Development Center or Small Business Development Center near you. Make sure to look into these local opportunities as they will typically be less competitive.

At my website, www.LeadHership.biz you can always purchase an organized list with application info readily available for 20+ grants open now. I also have one-on-one consulting available if you'd like more assistance with your business credit journey.

WEBSITE INFORMATION OFFERED

www.grants.gov
Federal funding opportunities published on Grants.gov are for organizations and entities supporting the development & management of government-funded programs and projects.

https://www.sba.gov/funding-programs/grants
SBA provides limited small business grants and grants to states and eligible community organizations to promote entrepreneurship.

www.mbda.gov
MBDA is the federal agency tasked with promoting the growth and competitiveness of minority-owned businesses. Applicants must be registered with D&B and Sam.gov and then they will have to look out for grant opportunities as they are posted. Grant competitions are regularly changing.

www.nmsdc.org
The National Minority Supplier Development Council provides a grant program known as the Business Consortium Fund, which is intended to support certified minority-owned businesses.

https://www.tgci.com/funding-sources
The TGCI connects you with funding resources by state, so you would select your state and see the funding opportunities there. They also provide grant writing training for your business.

https://www.grantwatch.com/Grantwatch.com
 is a site for Canada and the USA featuring almost 27,000 current grants, funding opportunities, awards, contracts, and archived grants (that will soon be available again) from foundations, corporations, federal, state, and local government funding sources.

HOW BUSINESSES USE CREDIT

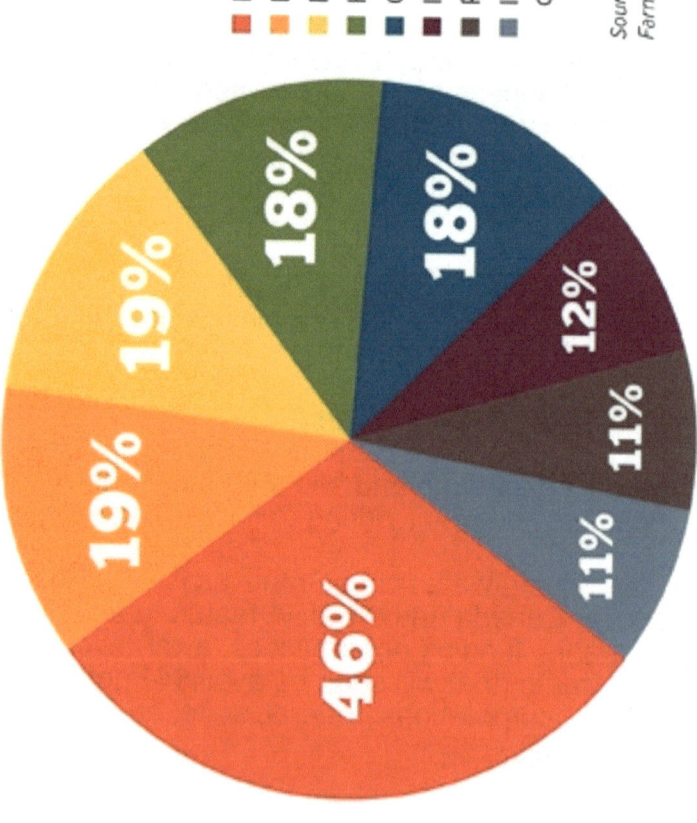

- Invest in new plant equipment: 46%
- Expand: 19%
- Maintain workforce: 19%
- Hire more employees: 18%
- Other: 18%
- Increase inventory: 12%
- R&D: 11%
- Increase employee compensation/benefits: 11%

Source: Fourth Quarter 2012 CBIA/Farmington Bank Credit Availability Survey

DISPUTE INACCURACIES ON YOUR BUSINESS CREDIT REPORTS

The next step to cleaning up your business credit is to dispute inaccuracies on your business credit report. This is important to do because often companies and even business credit bureaus make mistakes.

Here's how to dispute inaccuracies on your business credit reports:

1. Pull a copy of your business credit report from each major credit reporting agency (Dun & Bradstreet, Experian Business, and Equifax Small Business).
2. Review each report and highlight each inaccuracy. Check for how things are spelled, that the industry code is correct, dates align, trade lines are being reported accurately, and everything else looks correct.
3. Provide proof of the inaccuracies. You may have to contact vendors and even photocopy invoices and other financial statements to prove your case.
4. Mail, email, or fax back the highlighted reports and proof to the business credit bureaus to fix. It will usually take 30 days for these changes to reflect; however, Experian has a help portal on their website where changes can be made immediately.

Important: Privacy laws protect personal credit; however, business credit is not protected, and anyone can gain access to your business information.

NEGOTIATE TO REMOVE NEGATIVE MARKS ON YOUR BUSINESS CREDIT REPORT

Contact all vendors who have reported negative marks against your business credit and see if you can work something out with them to get them to remove the negative marks. This applies to both vendors you currently have and those who you've done business with in the past.

Here are some guidelines to help you:
- Ask if you make six months' payments on time if the creditor will take off the previous six months of negative marks. Tell them you're trying to repair your business credit, and they may wish to help).
- Contact old creditors and see what you can do to get them to remove the previous marks that have stained your credit. You may have to place an order with them, or you may get lucky, and they'll just willingly help you.
- Write letters to the business credit bureaus and fight the negative marks. Credit bureaus will often remove marks against you if you prove your case.
- When negotiating with creditors that you've wronged in the past, express how sorry you are and how you want to make things right with them. They are more likely to help you this way.

Recommended: Use Nav to monitor your business credit score and get up-to-date reports.

TYPES OF BUSINESS INSURANCE

There are various types of business insurance policies available for small business owners.

We'll explain the different types of insurance policies available for your business and help you pick the right insurer for your needs.

Recommended: Next Insurance is dedicated to matching small businesses with the right policy at the best price.

Business Insurance Types
Having the right policies in place can help protect businesses from risks and ensure their success in the long run.

Below is a breakdown of each commercial insurance type.

General Liability Insurance
General liability (GL) insurance is not only your first line of defense against insurable perils, but it's also an integral part of affordable business insurance options.

General liability insurance is a specific type of commercial liability insurance policy that shields a business from the financial strain of claims resulting from bodily injury, personal injury, or property damage. An essential component of affordable business insurance, it strikes a balance between cost and coverage.

In addition to these core coverages, general liability insurance can extend to include "advertising injury," which encompasses offenses such as copyright infringement and libel. By exploring affordable business insurance options, you can ensure broad protection without compromising your budget.

TYPES OF BUSINESS INSURANCE 2

Business Owner's Policy

A <u>business owner's policy</u> (BOP) is a combination of business liability insurance and business property insurance.
A BOP is often customized to the business it covers and is considered to be a comprehensive and affordable solution for small businesses.

Business Interruption Insurance
With <u>business interruption coverage</u>, you can feel confident that your business will be covered during incidents like major storms, problems with the local electrical grid, or even a hacking incident. This coverage is designed to protect your business during covered events and can replace the money you would have made or provide funds to operate in an alternate location temporarily.

Property Insurance
<u>Commercial property insurance</u> covers your building and its contents, as well as any resulting impact on your business income, in the event of damage due to fire, theft, or a natural disaster.

Business Content Insurance
<u>Business content insurance</u> covers items within your business from damage or theft. This insurance differs from property insurance and in that it does not cover the dwelling.
This insurance will ensure replacement of items such as belongings, furniture, equipment, inventory, and minimize operational disruption.

TYPES OF
BUSINESS INSURANCE 3

Product Liability Insurance
Product Liability Insurance will protect your business from claims of injury or damage caused by your products. This insurance can help cover costs from a lawsuit or legal fees.
Not all businesses will need this insurance, but if you sell physical products that have a higher risk of lawsuits, it is highly recommended.

Commercial Package
A commercial package policy combines various coverage types into one policy.
This policy can include property, general liability, business interruption, crime, and commercial auto insurance coverage.

Employment Practices Liability Insurance
Employment practices liability insurance (EPLI) safeguards businesses against employee lawsuits alleging inappropriate or unfair acts.
Even when done unknowingly, violating an employee's rights can result in significant expenses for the business. EPLI coverage is designed to protect businesses against such claims.

TYPES OF BUSINESS INSURANCE 4

Management Liability Insurance
Also known as directors and officers insurance (D&O), this policy provides protection to company executives and directors against claims made against them by employees, shareholders, or regulators.

This coverage protects the personal assets of these individuals and ensures they are not held responsible for the company's losses.

Errors and Omissions Insurance
Errors and omissions insurance (E&O) insurance is also known as **professional liability insurance**. This policy provides protection against financial losses due to errors, omissions, or negligence committed by the business or its employees.

Crime Coverage
Crime coverage is designed to protect businesses from various forms of criminal activity, such as fraud, forgery, and theft. This policy can cover employee theft or theft by outsiders.

Key Person Insurance
Key person insurance provides a financial payout to the company if the executive dies or becomes too disabled to work so the company can keep operating until it finds a replacement.

Protect Your Business Today
Finding the most affordable and comprehensive coverage starts with getting accurate quotes from highly rated providers.

Contact info@leadhership.biz for more information or a quote

TYPES OF BUSINESS INSURANCE 5

Self-Employed Business Insurance
Self-employed business insurance safeguards independent professionals against financial risks. It covers potential liability claims, property damages, and income losses. Tailored to specific risks, it ensures self-employed individuals can operate with confidence, knowing they're protected.

Public Liability Insurance
Public liability insurance covers a business against claims of personal injury or property damage caused to third parties. This insurance is essential for businesses interacting with the public, as it protects against costly legal expenses and damage reparations.

Business Hazard Insurance
Business hazard insurance protects businesses against physical damages from hazards such as fire, storms, theft, or vandalism. It covers the cost of repairing or replacing damaged physical assets, helping businesses recover quickly after a disaster.

Inventory Insurance
Inventory insurance covers a business's stock or inventory against loss, damage, or theft. This policy is crucial for businesses with substantial stock, ensuring they can recover quickly from any inventory-related setbacks and continue operations seamlessly.

Protect Your Business Today
Finding the most affordable and comprehensive coverage starts with getting accurate quotes from highly rated providers.

Contact info@leadhership.biz for more information or a quote

ABOUT THE AUTHOR

Atneciv Rodriguez is a serial entrepreneur whose passion is to help other entrepreneurs build, grow and sustain in Business, Finances, and Mindset. She empowers her readers to trust their intuition and create their own opportunities and fulfill whatever their desires are.

With her system of Business and finances, she has helped hundreds of people especially women bring their passions to life and held them accountable to put their ideas into action.

Atneciv has been professionally certified and licensed in Life Coaching, Business Consulting, Financial Literacy, Credit, Insurance, Taxes, Investments, and in Esthetics for her other businesses.

For more information visit www.LeadHership.biz

Made in the USA
Columbia, SC
11 November 2024